To all the lovers out there

Hey there lovers!

Relationships are meant to be FUN. So let's have some.

You make up your own rules as you go. Choose your favourite activities and take it from there.

Set some time aside to turn off the digital devices and have some fun with this book.

When was the
last time we had a big night out?

Lover A:

_____

_____

_____

_____

_____

Lover B:

_____

_____

_____

_____

_____

Draw It

Draw the first time we met in a comic.

Lover A

Draw It

Draw the first time we met in a comic.

Lover B

Pop Quiz

Give yourself a point for each question you get right.

1. What's your partner's favourite colour?

2. What's your partner's dream car?

3. Does your partner have any hidden talents?

4. What's your partner's favourite nickname for you?

5. When was the last time your partner cried?

6. What's your partner's favourite past time?

7. How would your partner describe you?

8. What's your partner's favourite song?

9. What annoys your partner most?

10. What dish could your partner eat every single day?

11. What's your partner's favourite song?

12. What makes your partner laugh out loud?

13. What's relaxing to your partner?

14. What's your partner's idea of the perfect day?

15. Which part of your body does your partner love the most?

Moments

List three of your partner's favourite assets =)

Lover A:

_____

_____

_____

_____

_____

Lover B:

_____

_____

_____

_____

_____

Activity

Watch your partner doing something they love from afar.

In one of Ester Perel's Ted Talks, she shares when partners find the other the most attractive. It's when one is observing them from a distance. Watch your partner play a sports match if they love sports. Go to a party and go mingle from opposite sides of the room. Have them watch you dance.

Writing prompt

Finish the sentence.
I never thought we'd be...

Lover A:

_____

_____

_____

_____

_____

Lover B:

_____

_____

_____

_____

_____

Draw It
Your partner as a superhero

Partner's superhero name:

Super power:

Draw It
Your partner as a superhero

Partner's superhero name:

Super power:

Pop Quiz

Give yourself a point for each question you get right.

1. What's your partner's favourite emoji?

2. Name the catch phrase your partner always uses

3. What's your partner's biggest pet peeve?

4. Who was your partner's first crush?

5. Does your partner like public displays of affection?

6. What's one thing that would make your partner's day?

7. What's one thing your partner can't get enough of?

8. What's your partner's karaoke tune?

9. Who does your partner admire the most?

10. Is your partner more like dad or mom?

11. What would make your partner happy today?

12. What's your partner's least favourite colour?

13. Did your partner have a childhood pet?

14. What's one cause your partner is most passionate about?

15. What's one article of clothing your partner will never ever throw away?

Moments

Write about your favourite memory with your partner

Lover A:

_____

_____

_____

_____

_____

Lover B:

_____

_____

_____

_____

_____

Activity
Pictionary

Take turns choosing a word/event/thing that you and your partner share. Now have the other person guess the word. You can draw it out.

Writing prompt

Write down a list of things you want to do
with your partner

Lover A:

_____

_____

_____

_____

_____

_____

_____

_____

_____

Writing prompt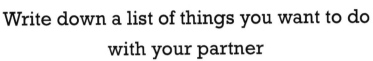

Write down a list of things you want to do with your partner

Lover B:

_____

_____

_____

_____

_____

_____

_____

_____

Draw It
The nine box: Partner A

Share nine things that describe who you are

The car that best describes you	One piece of article that represents you	Your favourite music album
A dish you can eat every day	People you love	A decade you'd live in
Biggest fear	Which animal would you be?	Four people you'd like to invite to dinner

Draw It

The nine box: Partner A

Share nine things that describe who you are

Draw It
The nine box: Partner B

Share nine things that describe who you are

The car that best describes you	One piece of article that represents you	Your favourite music album
A dish you can eat every day	People you love	A decade you'd live in
Biggest fear	Which animal would you be?	Four people you'd like to invite to dinner

Draw It

The nine box: Partner B

Share nine things that describe who you are

Solve it
Word combos
How many words can you create from each of
the above? i.e. In relationship, you can create
words like ship, rip, hip…

Relationship

Valentine

Lover

Quotables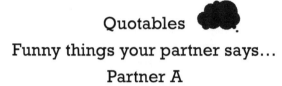

Funny things your partner says...

Partner A

What's one phrase or word your partner uses that always makes you laugh?

_____

_____

_____

The silliest thing you've ever heard your partner say

_____

_____

_____

Quotables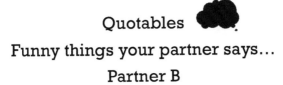

Funny things your partner says...

Partner B

What's one phrase or word your
partner uses that always makes you
laugh?

_____

_____

_____

The silliest thing you've ever heard
your partner say

_____

_____

_____

Draw It

Draw a caricature of your partner

Draw It

Draw a caricature of your partner

Couples Pictionary

Take a few sheets of paper.
Take turns writing facts about your marriage like your favourite takeaway place, where you first met, your wedding date...etc. Have one person draw a slip of paper and draw it for the other person to guess.

Writing prompt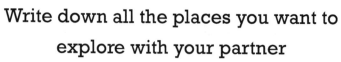

Write down all the places you want to explore with your partner

Lover A:

_____

_____

_____

_____

_____

_____

_____

_____

Writing prompt

Write down all the places you want to
explore with your partner

Lover B:

_____

_____

_____

_____

_____

_____

_____

_____

_____

Draw It. ✏️

Write your partner a love note…in emojis.

Partner A

Draw It.
Write your partner a love note…in emojis.
Partner B

Real Talk 📣

So many ways to love you...

List 10 things your partner can do to woo you

Partner A

_____

_____

_____

_____

_____

_____

_____

_____

_____

_____

Real Talk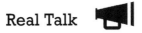

So many ways to love you…

List 10 things your partner can do to woo you

Partner B

_____

_____

_____

_____

_____

_____

_____

_____

_____

_____

Romantic Tic Tac Toe

It's just like the game you know but better. One person will have x's. The other will have o's. Place either an x or o in each box and follow the instructions.

Give your partner a strip tease	Kiss for 7 minutes straight	Get naked
Give your partner a naked cuddle	Choose a dare for your partner to act out	Have a staring contest
Take off your partner's clothes (if they're not already naked)	Tell your partner your secret fantasy	Lock lips

Romantic Tic Tac Toe

Your Scorecard

Game 1	
Game 2	
Game 3	
Game 4	
Game 5	

The Lemon Game

The objective of the game is to transfer a handful of lemons into a bowl. The catch is that you and your partner need to do this without using your hands. Once you've mastered your technique, time yourself to see how quickly you can complete the exercise. No cheating. =)

Draw It.

Map out your dream home. Draw the floor plan.

Partner A

Draw It.

Map out your dream home. Draw the floor plan.

Partner B

Real Talk 📣

Fill in the blanks
Partner A

I love you the most when...

_____

I'm so proud of...

_____

A love song to describe our relationship
would be...

_____

Three things I admire about you...

_____

I knew it was love when...

_____

Real Talk

Fill in the blanks

Partner B

I love you the most when...

_____

I'm so proud of...

_____

A love song to describe our relationship
would be...

_____

Three things I admire about you...

_____

I knew it was love when...

_____

Writing prompt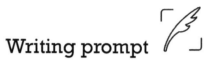

Come up with a bucket list of things to do

Lover A:

Writing prompt

Come up with a bucket list of things to do

Lover B:

_____

_____

_____

_____

_____

_____

_____

_____

_____

The Love Memory Game

Re-create the tiles on this page and the next (or just cut them from this page). Match two cards together and follow the instructions.

Kiss Me	Kiss Me	Hug Me
Hug Me	5 minute massage	5 minute massage
Show me some love	Show me some love	xoxo

The Love Memory Game

Re-create the tiles below or just cut them from this page. Match two cards together and follow the instructions.

xoxo	Truth or Dare	Truth or Dare
Dance	Dance	Cuddle Me
Cuddle Me	Get Naked	Get Naked

Love Memory Game

Your Scorecard

Game 1	
Game 2	
Game 3	
Game 4	
Game 5	

Love Notes

Write your partner love notes.

Optional: cut them out into strips and put them in a glass jar for him/her to read for the next three days.

Partner A

Love Notes

Write your partner love notes.

Optional: cut them out into strips and put them in a

glass jar for him/her to read for the next three days.

Partner B

Writing prompt

Things we should do next date night

Lover A:

_____

_____

_____

_____

_____

_____

_____

_____

Writing prompt

Things we should do next date night

Lover B:

_____

_____

_____

_____

_____

_____

_____

_____

Would you rather ❓

Lover A:

☐ Go on a camping adventure or holiday at a 5 star resort? ☐

☐ Be covered in fur or covered in scales? ☐

☐ Have a key to any city or a get out of jail card? ☐

☐ Live in a small home in a great area or a mansion in the middle of nowhere? ☐

☐ Have the secret power to be invisible or listen to people's inner thoughts? ☐

☐ Have an easy job that pays fair wages or a job that's challenging and something you're passionate about? ☐

☐ Have a chef that cooks for you daily or a driver that takes you everywhere daily? ☐

☐ Dance to every song you hear or sing every song you hear? ☐

☐ Be caught farting or lying? ☐

Would you rather ❓

Lover B:

☐ Go on a camping adventure or holiday at a 5 star resort? ☐

☐ Be covered in fur or covered in scales? ☐

☐ Have a key to any city or a get out of jail card? ☐

☐ Live in a small home in a great area or a mansion in the middle of nowhere? ☐

☐ Have the secret power to be invisible or listen to people's inner thoughts? ☐

☐ Have an easy job that pays fair wages or a job that's challenging and something you're passionate about? ☐

☐ Have a chef that cooks for you daily or a driver that takes you everywhere daily? ☐

☐ Dance to every song you hear or sing every song you hear? ☐

☐ Be caught farting or lying? ☐

Writing prompt

Brag about your partner. Let's say...your partner
was going to win an award for being her/him.
And now let's pretend you are presenting this

Lover A:

_____

_____

_____

_____

_____

_____

_____

_____

Writing prompt

Brag about your partner. Let's say...your partner
was going to win an award for being her/him.
And now let's pretend you are presenting this

Lover B:

_____

_____

_____

_____

_____

_____

_____

_____

Draw It

Draw your favourite date and have the other person guess it.

Partner A

Draw It

Draw your favourite date and have the other
person guess it.

Partner B

List 10 things you've learned about relationships

Lover A:

_____

_____

_____

_____

_____

_____

_____

_____

Writing prompt

List 10 things you've learned about

relationships

Lover B:

_____

_____

_____

_____

_____

_____

_____

_____

_____

Romantic Tic Tac Toe

It's just like the game you know but better. One person will have x's. The other will have o's. Place either an x or o in each box and follow the instructions.

Tell your partner a secret	Truth or Dare	Sing a duet
Have a tickle fight	Give your partner a sensual kiss	Have a staring contest
Kiss your partner on the cheek	Give your partner a quick 5 minute massage	Give your partner a hug

Romantic Tic Tac Toe

Your Scorecard

Draw It

Draw what your life looks like in 10 years
Partner A

Draw It

Draw what your life looks like in 10 years
Partner B

Writing prompt

Write a love poem and recite it to your partner. You can make it romantic or silly.

Lover A:

_____

_____

_____

_____

_____

_____

_____

_____

Writing prompt

Write a love poem and recite it to your partner. You can make it romantic or silly.

Lover B:

_____

_____

_____

_____

_____

_____

_____

_____

Would you rather ?
Lover A:

☐ Have looks over brains? ☐

☐ Be incredibly rich or incredibly fit? ☐

☐ Eat one dish every day for the rest of your life or a different dish every day? ☐

☐ Live on a boat or in the wild? ☐

☐ Be telepathic or psychic? ☐

☐ Wear a bathing suit to work or wedding dress to work everyday? ☐

☐ Be a super star or super athlete? ☐

☐ Be a mermaid/merman or a cave woman/cave man? ☐

☐ Be friends with a bear or a wolf pack? ☐

Would you rather ?

Lover B:

☐ **Have looks over brains?** ☐

☐ Be incredibly rich or incredibly fit? ☐

☐ Eat one dish every day for the rest of your life or a different dish every day? ☐

☐ Live on a boat or in the wild? ☐

☐ Be telepathic or psychic? ☐

☐ Wear a bathing suit to work or wedding dress to work everyday? ☐

☐ Be a super star or super athlete? ☐

☐ Be a mermaid/merman or a cave woman/cave man? ☐

☐ Be friends with a bear or a wolf pack? ☐

Real Talk

Fill in the blanks

Partner A

I feel the most vulnerable when...

_____

Things are worry me right now...

_____

I always want to know...

_____

When we argue I...

_____

What makes me most happy is...

_____

Real Talk 📢

Fill in the blanks
Partner B

I feel the most vulnerable when...

_____

Things are worry me right now...

_____

I always want to know...

_____

When we argue I...

_____

What makes me most happy is...

_____

Date Night Ideas

Come up with as many date ideas as you can.

_____

_____

_____

_____

_____

_____

_____

_____

_____

Date Night Ideas

Come up with as many date ideas as you can.

_____

_____

_____

_____

_____

_____

_____

_____

The shoe game

Answer the following questions with honesty. Sit back to back. Ask the question out loud and if you think you fit any of the questions below, put up your shoe. Turn around and see if your partner put their shoe up or not.

1. Who is the pickier eater?

2. Who is the better driver?

4. Who is the better cook?

6. Who is the messiest?

7. Who spends more time getting ready?

8. Who is the loudest?

10. Who is the nerd?

12. Who is the most competitive?

13. Who is the most emotional?

14. Who is most likely to say something they'll regret 30 seconds later?

Writing prompt

List 10 things you and your partner haven't done

Lover A:

_____

_____

_____

_____

_____

_____

_____

_____

_____

Writing prompt

List 10 things you and your partner haven't done

Lover B:

_____

_____

_____

_____

_____

_____

_____

_____

_____

Two truths and a lie

Firstly, come up with a prize for the winner.
Each person comes up with two truths about them
and a lie. The other person has to guess which of
those statements are a lie. Best two out of three
wins.

Draw It

Draw your idea of the dream date
Partner A

Draw It

Draw your idea of the dream date
Partner B

Writing prompt

List 10 things you and your partner can do to improve your relationship

Lover A:

_____

_____

_____

_____

_____

_____

_____

_____

_____

Writing prompt

List 10 things you and your partner can do to improve your relationship

Lover B:

_____

_____

_____

_____

_____

_____

_____

_____

_____

Reflection

List three things you've learned from finishing this activity book

Lover A:

_____

_____

_____

_____

Lover B:

_____

_____

_____

_____

Made in the USA
San Bernardino, CA
21 May 2020